FARM ANIMALS

DONKEYS

by Michelle Hasselius

Consultant: Dr. Mark Z. Johnson
Department of Animal Science
Oklahoma State University

CAPSTONE PRESS
a capstone imprint

Pebble Plus is published by Capstone Press,
1710 Roe Crest Drive, North Mankato, Minnesota 56003.
www.mycapstone.com

Library of Congress Cataloging-in-Publication Data
Names: Hasselius, Michelle M., 1981– author.
Title: Donkeys / by Michelle Hasselius.
Other titles: Pebble plus. Farm animals.
Description: North Mankato, Minnesota : Capstone Press, [2017] | Series:
Pebble plus. Farm animals | Includes bibliographical references and index.
Identifiers: LCCN 2015051423
ISBN 9781515709251 (library binding) | ISBN 9781515709640 (pbk.) | ISBN 9781515710998 (ebook pdf)
Subjects: LCSH: Donkeys—Juvenile literature.
Classification: LCC SF361 .H37 2017 | DDC 636.1/82—dc23
LC record available at http://lccn.loc.gov/2015051423

Editorial Credits
Michelle Hasselius, editor; Kayla Rossow, designer; Pam Mitsakos, media researcher;
Katy LaVigne, production specialist

Photo Credits
Shutterstock: Andrei Ovasko, 6–7, ChiccoDodiFC, 19, Daniel Wilson, 13, Dennis W. Donohue, 9, DragoNika, cover,
Eky Studio, (back cover background), Elena Larina, 16–17, Elenamiv, 22 (background), Elisa Locci, 10–11, Germano
Poli, 15, Kookkai_nak, 1 (background), Menna, 1; Thinkstock: jtyler, 5, Purestock, 20–21

Note to Parents and Teachers

The Farm Animals series supports national science standards related to life science. This
book describes and illustrates donkeys. The images support early readers in understanding
the text. The repetition of words and phrases helps early readers learn new words. This
book also introduces early readers to subject-specific vocabulary words, which are defined
in the Glossary section. Early readers may need assistance to read some words and to use
the Table of Contents, Glossary, Read More, Internet Sites, and Index sections of the book.

Printed and bound in China.
007708

Table of Contents

Meet the Donkeys

Hee-haw! The donkeys bray loudly on the farm. The sound can be heard from far away. Donkeys bray to communicate with each other.

Donkeys have shaggy coats.

Many donkeys are gray.

But they can also be black,

brown, red-brown, or white.

Some are even spotted.

There are three types of donkeys. Miniatures are less than 36 inches (0.9 meter) tall. Standards are 36 to 54 inches tall. Mammoths are more than 54 inches (1.4 m) tall.

miniature donkey

There are more than 44 million donkeys in the world. Many live on farms. Donkeys weigh up to 570 pounds (258 kilograms). They can live 25 years or more.

Adults and Babies

Donkeys grow up on the farm.

Male donkeys are called jacks.

Females are called jennies.

Foals are baby donkeys.

They stand and walk soon after birth.

jenny

foal

13

On the Farm

Donkeys spend their time in fenced pastures. They eat grass and hay. Donkeys also need a stable or barn. It protects donkeys from rain, wind, and snow.

Donkeys are strong. They can
carry heavy loads on their backs.
Donkeys can also pull carts.
Long ago farmers used donkeys
to plow fields.

A Donkey's Role

Today farmers use donkeys to protect sheep, cattle, and goats. Donkeys do not like foxes and dogs. Donkeys bray and chase them away from the herds.

Donkeys can be kept as pets.
Farmers also use donkeys
to calm nervous horses.
The donkey stays with the
horse in the stable and pasture.

Glossary

bray—to make a loud, harsh noise

coat—an animal's fur or wool

communicate—to share information, thoughts, or feelings

herd—a large group of animals that lives or moves together

nervous—scared or timid

pasture—land where farm animals eat grass and exercise

plow—to turn over soil before seeds are planted

stable—a building or part of a building where farm animals are kept; animals such as donkeys, horses, and cattle use stables

Read More

Bailer, Darice. *Donkeys.* Animals. New York: Marshall Cavendish Benchmark, 2012.

Spilsbury, Louise, and Richard Spilsbury. *A Nature Walk on the Farm.* Nature Walks. Chicago: Heinemann Library, 2015.

Yasuda, Anita. *Donkeys.* Animals on the Farm. New York: AV2 by Weigl, 2013.

Internet Sites

FactHound offers a safe, fun way to find Internet sites related to this book. All of the sites on FactHound have been researched by our staff.

Here's all you do:

Visit *www.facthound.com*

Type in this code: 9781515709251

Check out projects, games and lots more at
www.capstonekids.com

Index